Standing On Marbles

Three Leader Types In Verse And Imagery

Karol M. Wasylyshyn, PsyD

Illustrated by
Richard McKnight

Philadelphia

DEDICATION

For all my executive clients—
from your letting me in, all of this has poured out

and for

Ulys ("Duke") H. Yates,
without you, my poet's voice would still be still

and for

Frank Masterpasqua
because you taught me about giving away psychology

Published by TrueNorth Press, Philadelphia, PA

Wasylyshyn, Karol, M., McKnight, Richard. Standing On Marbles: Three Leader Types In
Verse And Imagery
Philadelphia: TrueNorth Press, 2011.
p. : ill. ; cm.
Summary: Poetic vignettes revealing three leadership types from 300 case files of an
executive coach.
ISBN: 978-0-9824683-3-3
Library of Congress Control Number: 2010941480
First Edition

This book is available at discount when purchased in quantity (15 or more copies). To
inquire, go to TrueNorthPress.com.

Book design, jacket design, and typesetting by Richard McKnight.
Set in Didot, Brisa, and Gil Sans.

Contents

An Invitation

STANDING ON MARBLES PROVIDES AN uncommon look into the psyches of some of the most extraordinary business leaders in America. These leaders represent every global sector and a broad array of industries. They also represent a wide spectrum of leadership behavior that I have identified and verified through research as three distinct leadership types: *Remarkable, Perilous, and Toxic.*

I realize that my identification of these three leadership types may seem simplistic and perhaps even arrogant. My intent is not to over-simplify or to stereotype leaders nor to proffer these types as a defini-tive representation of leadership styles but rather to examine a truth that most of us who have worked in business organizations know well: there are great leaders, so-so leaders, and terrible ones, too.

With this identification of three leader types, I have put a descriptive stake in the sand. I could have named these leaders colors. I could have named them trees, or animals, or cars. The names of these three leader types matter less than this: running a business is hard and messy and it is often very unsteady—like standing on marbles. Some business execu-tives can do this well; some can learn to do it better; and some will never lead well. *Standing on Marbles* is a psychologically-informed attempt to help you understand—in a way that is distinct from most books on lead-ers—the differences among leaders most everyone knows.

My hope is that you will benefit from understanding these three types of leaders, both for your own growth and because you probably have a boss and understanding him or her better can't hurt. Your un-derstanding will emerge through the stories written here about these three types of leaders—stories based on real people who represent each type. These stories are purposely told through poetry thus leaving all interpretation up to you.

While you may turn to the Commentaries at the back of this book to learn of the genesis of each poem, I invite you to stay principally with your own thoughts. I invite you to linger in the white space surrounding each poem—a place where you can reflect about leadership. The person or moment that catalyzed each poem matters infinitely less than what is evoked for you from each story. How you use your reactions to them and the conversations they may spawn with others about leaders is the vehicle for deepening your understanding.

In the spare lines of these poems we are reminded of leaders' distinctive talents and of their torments as they struggle to maintain balance in the unsteadiness of 21st century business conditions. Their efforts, as revealed through these poems, may comfort, startle, or even stun you. You may have a fond reverie of a Remarkable boss; you may shudder at the memory of an unpredictable Perilous boss; or you may be reminded of the irrational tirades of a Toxic boss. After reading this book, perhaps you can place all of these experiences with leaders into a fuller perspective.

Finally, I am reminded of a conversation I had with the American poet, Ulys H. Yates, who said, "The poet makes the specific universal." So if you think you recognize yourself in one of these poems, remember you are simultaneously distinct and representative of others who share your leadership type. Also, remember that you are not consistently one of these types. Circumstances can influence your moving along the continuum of Remarkable, Perilous and Toxic behavior—in both your work and personal life. Your special gift to whomever you lead or love is to be Remarkable most of the time. My sincere hope is that *Standing on Marbles* can help you get there.

Karol M. Wasylyshyn, PsyD
Philadelphia, PA
Winter, 2010

The Desert

I work in a desert that's parched
and cracked and relentlessly beige.
People get encrusted in sand here,
their ideas scorched, bleached or battered
unless they reach an oasis but even then,
real danger lurks at the well
its stones chipped, and stained by the blood of others
others who lurk mumbling incoherent, lying in wait ...
just to throw scorpions under the bench.

I work in a desert that's as sudden
and inescapable
as the most *remarkable* people here—
white linen jackets and hats
hats with long canvas flaps down the back
lest the sun bake them dry.
But they'll not be baked or
distracted by the elements;
instead, they drink the fresh water I pour,
and peel the oranges I've
pulled from a deeper pocket.
We feast in unison.

I work in a desert that's searing by day
and numbing by night.
Camels carry the *perilous* nomads here—
these nomads half warrior, half ghost
tumble onto the sand

they are thirsty, they are crawling,
they are heaving into the heat,
they have good reason to rest but
they are scraping toward their destinations,
destinations they reach but
are never quite full enough.

I work in a desert that's as harsh
and repetitive
as the *toxic* people here —
people who wrap their heads in cloth
when the sandstorms come,
cloth so thick I can't cut the slits for them to see;
cloths wrapped so tightly that when
the deafening winds roar
they cannot hear — not even their names
names that I'm screaming from the table.

I work in a desert that's parched
and cracked and relentlessly beige.
Through the winds and the sand and the heat
I still see the people who sent me here ...
seasoned stewards of nomads and ghosts;
for them I leave a palette of oils,
an expectant canvas, and a brush —
for whilst I've been a guest, they must
keep painting the sands vibrantly.

Three Leadership Types

SEVERAL YEARS AGO, I PILED 300 executive coaching case files on a conference table and asked myself: Do the behaviors of these business leaders represent any particular patterns? After analyzing the data contained in those records—life history, psychological testing, organization leadership competency data, and interview notes, I concluded that there were indeed patterns. From these patterns, I identified three leadership types and named them *Remarkable, Perilous, and Toxic.*

The results of recent research conducted with my colleague, Dr. Hal Shorey, Assistant Professor at Widener University's Institute for Graduate Clinical Psychology, have shown that these three leadership types are empirically distinct based on two commonly used psychometric measures: the *BarOn Emotional Quotient Inventory* (EQ-i) and the *Revised NEO Personality Inventory* (NEO PI-R).

Before I provide brief descriptions of these types, an important—and I hope instructive—caveat: leaders are not locked into a particular type, including you, if you are a leader. Rather, business leaders are dynamic and move, at least to some degree, on the continuum between Remarkable and Toxic. The degree to which they move along this continuum is influenced most significantly by their personalities and, in my experience, their tolerance for stress.

In other words, how leaders behave at a given time is determined by the confluence of work and personal events. Depending on the nature of these events, their confidence in being able to manage them effectively, and their ability to learn from experience, leaders will behave at the top, middle or bottom level of their abilities—much like a football player on any given Sunday. For example, while stellar business executives are Remarkable most of the time, circumstances can—and do—have adverse effects that can pull them toward Perilous or even Toxic behavior.

The Remarkable Leader

Remarkable business leaders possess distinctive intellectual, interpersonal and leadership competencies. Intellectually, their agile minds facilitate excellent analysis and problem-solving. Readily able to distill complex data, they get to the core of issues quickly. They recognize patterns, look around the corners, and influence rapid decision-making. They are emblematic of what I have termed total brain leadership—that rare combination of high IQ (innate ability) and equally high EQ (emotional intelligence).

It is the emotional intelligence (EQ) of Remarkable leaders that makes them standout so clearly. EQ is defined as the ability to discern one's own emotions as well as those of others and to be able to use that emotional awareness to help achieve objectives either personal or work-related. Leaders with high EQ are interpersonally gifted and can channel their feelings effectively—both positive (e.g. happiness, excitement, passion,) and negative (e.g. anger, frustration, impatience). Further, given their attunement to others, they are able to address people's real concerns, needs, and aspirations. Remarkable leaders are usually high-touch people who know how and when to display genuine empathy. Finally, based on their authentic way of relating to people both inside and outside their organizations, they form relationships that are personal and lasting—not just task-oriented and situational.

Remarkable leaders possess an array of essential leadership competencies that include visionary thinking, strategic planning and execution, customer focus, innovation management, the ability to form and inspire high performing teams, driving results, and a significant degree of executive presence. Executive presence refers to their steadiness under pressure, excellent communication skills, optimism, tenacity, and resilience (especially in the wake of bad business results). In short, their success is heightened by their personal brand of charisma.

The Perilous Leader

Perilous leaders are, for the most part, just as talented as Remarkable leaders. However, there are certain behavioral nuances related to their relentless frustration, critical self-perceptions, and often judgmental interactions with others that erode their overall effectiveness.

Intellectually, they are often gifted but unable to fully apply the power of their cognitive strengths because they get distracted by organizational political issues, mired in procrastination, and paralyzed in the midst of decision making. Sometimes described by their teams as "chaos makers," they vacillate on direction thus creating more confusion than clarity about strategy and strategic priorities. Because they can prefer problem solving via a solitary process, key would-be partners are left feeling excluded or disempowered.

While they can possess at least a moderate degree of emotional intelligence, Perilous leaders are erratic in their ability to tap into positive emotions as a motivational resource. Further, they do not typically express sufficient empathy toward others, and their relationships tend to be cool and distant. Dark periods of self-doubt and episodes of volatility further limit the ability of these leaders to connect with others inside the organization. However, they are usually able to control this behavior, enabling them to establish rapport with key external stakeholders. Their underlying insecurity and/or self-limiting, destructive patterns of behavior (e.g., excessive drinking, philandering, and extreme workaholism) can further undermine their accomplishments.

Perilous leaders can be as talented as their Remarkable peers on classic leadership competencies especially strategic thinking, driving accountability, and achieving results. Herein, perhaps, is the real sadness pertaining to Perilous leaders: certain compulsive behaviors sabotage their full potential. Further, the relentlessness of their harsh self-criticism leaves them embittered about never having achieved that potential. Their persistent criticisms of others—especially their leadership team members—can leave talented employees feeling de-motivated, disillusioned, and detached from the organization. In the end, Perilous leaders can pose perils for others but they are most perilous to themselves. They are destined to live lives in which work contentment and personal happiness will inevitably elude them. In short, they are unrequited in both love and work.

The Toxic Leader

Toxic leaders can be brilliant and technically strong but their intellectual strengths tend to be comprised seriously by psychological issues. These leaders are not interested in self-development and can shut down completely in the face of demanding business conditions that require a shift in strategy. They can become explosive or otherwise resistant to change experiencing any suggestion of the need for their development or change as an indictment of their capabilities.

Interpersonally, Toxic leaders experience significant difficulties. Their needs to be admired, heard, and lauded above others dominate their abilities to connect with or to be present for others. Unlike the productive narcissism of the Remarkable or Perilous leader, these leaders' needs for ego-boosting, attention, and affirmation, coupled with their often vicious competitive instincts, make them unpredictable and dangerous. Since they possess very limited EQ, they cannot see themselves or their impact on others objectively. Toxic leaders are seriously deficit in the ability to manage or channel their emotions effectively, especially hostility. Their capacity for empathy is negligible. Further, their grandiosity and self-absorption severely compromise their ability to form trusting, lasting relationships—either at work or in their personal lives.

While they may possess certain leadership competencies, the overall picture is spotty. Serious psychological issues—including suspiciousness of others that can border on paranoia—erode their ability to use these competencies fully. Their flawed judgment gives rise to inappropriate language and behavior in the workplace, as well as impetuous decision-making. In the end, the toxicity of these leaders can contaminate corporate cultures with negativity, greed, and predatory behavior intended to get their insatiable needs met.

In the following pages, you will meet Remarkable, Perilous, and Toxic leaders—presented in free verse and imagery. While these words and images may highlight beliefs you already hold about business leaders, they should also prompt fresh insights regarding the haunting complexities of business leadership.

I.

REMARKABLE
Leaders

The Solidity of Fog

He would step into it early
as it tumbled low over the land
but high enough to envelop him
morning scapular
that he could embrace
press onto himself
kiss as a totem
certainty in the quiet,
clarity in the calm
as he worked the right problem
alone in this sudden place
mysterious in its habits
and the fog
the fog was the only
thing
he
could
trust
completely.

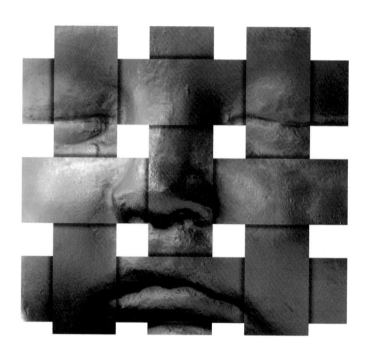

Deal Weaver

Only he caught that snag of a word

word dropped onto the table just as they rose …

rose numbed from the dinner and headed for sleep

sleep now fully trumped for him by the weaving

fast weaving of the snag, loosened thread

threading it tightly … back into place

right place

before anyone could pull it

pull it in the morning

… unraveling the deal completely.

Boss Titillated

After their first dinner, she spent days
in a sudden fury of distraction
during which she tasted three new wines,
listened to Astrid Gilberto,
and contemplated the purchase of a
backless Goddess dress she'd probably never wear.
Sleep came in staggered bursts of tossing
and everything smelled like fresh rain
even in the elevator cab
where she'd spy him from the back most mornings
beautiful, balding, bulging in all the right places
and once with a shaving cut near where
his jaw jutted out from the ear lobe,
ear lobe that she wanted to lick
and suck off his head right then,
before they met to discuss his new responsibilities.

Killer Bees

There ... yes! He strikes the wounded beehive again

hanging high in the roof's throat, baseball hard to its gut

broken bees buzzing and bewildered.

Contented sleeping later under night's indigo coverlet

same indigo color as legs, legs pulled up in

fetal comma or semi colon if you count the head

now safe in a dream ... away in the indigo

deeper, thicker safe dreaming place where

once his heart split open releasing

a flight of bloodied bees

that infested the house

and stung his father senseless.

On The River

One river twisted,
endless churning within,
tangled debris deep below
blocking his motion,
distorting all sight,
muddying the night sheet
encasing him in questions and doubt …

Until he stumbled ashore
and glimpsed another
crystalline surface
poised for its time to receive him
soon,
he having honored what's done,
and knowing any more of it would kill him.

Quiet simple getaway
to his silent morning rendezvous
luminous date
with a fish from his past
taunting, salmon
resplendent on the river
awaiting
their most exuberant dancing.

Biscuit

Even as he left again, she felt contented

knowing that this was just another going,

an opening in the forest, a comma, a graceful turn,

a good wine to drink slowly after the kids went to bed.

His voice had been soothing and warm that morning

like a hot buttered biscuit sliding down her throat.

She wanted to slide down his,

feed him in the stale air of his bland hotel

and help speed his career to its proud ending—

with just enough jam left …

for their sweet reinvention.

Mourning In Kyoto

I see her gazing into the ryokan garden ...

bittersweet reverie I think

until she says,

"It takes a lifetime

to just sit and stare watching

watching

a rain drop

drop

from one leaf

to another below."

Empty Next

We escaped it again, didn't we?
We Freudian-slipped nest to next –
do you remember, an hour ago at lunch
that quick creeping up to it
that semi-glow feel of it
that open, brave dew of it
like we were really on it?
Then the fading … fast fading away from it;
we are strong masters of elusion you and I
even knowing It is the silken thread
to open, or lift the heart anew.
If you lie still, I will pull it gently through your throat
this will not hurt,
there will be no blood
it will be a sudden sliding and
when you see it—NO, when you hold it
it will become your kite's string and
you will fly—fly mighty from your familiar nest;
empty will become full again.
Let me pull it … let me pull it …
let me pull it now, and we can soar together.

Standing on Marbles

In my files "sexual harassment" sits

between "schizophrenia" and "succession planning"

a reminder perhaps that hard-striving women

aren't any crazier than hard striving men

they're just more remarkable …

having traded glass ceilings for marbles.

Standing steady on marbles

twirling ten plates simultaneously

smooth as granite, Teflon, and tenderness, too

these business warriors,

fierce working Amazon women.

So tell me—what's the difference

between a good bitch and a bad bitch?

Slow Dance In A Snow Storm

She wanted to slow dance
in a snow storm
northern Maine white out
burying them in powder but ...
still keeping it
close.

Closer and closer it came
... muffled song closer
revival enough with
the smell of the snow and
the thought of his motion
There.

This would keep her going
when the going got stalled
Kennedy, Heathrow
same weary colleagues
throwing back beer and
grinding the numbers.

The numbers ... grinding;
she had all the numbers
like a good dance
tight ... and smooth
with just enough snow
to keep it interesting.

Duende

The words fall into each other rolling over and over
smooth, steady ball bouncing between them
the room drenched in an amber light
as their breathing ... their breathing keeps moving
moving in a rhythm soothing the weight of the hour
and their eyes, their eyes locked onto each other whilst
dismissing the assembled papers on the table
the papers masquerading as real information.

Neither one of them notices the fly—
big buzzing house fly that's broken through,
it careens from window to ceiling to wall unable to land
but they never see it—so intent in their words, words buzzing
buzzing back and forth intensity and unity with the fly
for they are strangers, too but their words, their words keep
falling
landing into each other rolling over and over into the amber
light.

Nothing will be left unsaid ...
there is no perch for confusion,
no berth for resting, no corner for escaping the words
all the words are being said—and heard
... heard over and over as each provides a bench for the other.
They are stepping from moss to wet rock
without slipping,

they are building a bridge to the table cleared
and set anew.
They have maintained reverence for the past,
shed truth on the present,
and staged the future for change: coveted vermilion gate.
This was not the usual performance review.

II.
PERILOUS
Leaders

Riffed Off

Take down the plaques from his wall,
remove all the mirrors, too
he will not greet himself there;
a riffed name on the dreaded list now
now notified, wrapped in a package,
badge taken
he taken over and emptied out
into an hour of cavernous confusion.
Today is the last day, worst day
incomprehensible day
cruelest day
twenty-nine years of days
condensed into flashbacks
ricocheting through him.
Kubler-Ross stages
cacophonous sweat at night
nightmare,
night shirt
all twisted
night stand cracked
sorrowful kick
quick shot of pain
aimless, silent
night

of carols unremembered
drinking coffee in his underwear
a shot at lunch, pounding the small glass down,
down on the wood
wooden management
messed up
bad.

Night Moves

Two martinis and a bottle

of Chardonnay later,

he's as loose as rain,

as expansive as paint,

and ready to sleep for the first time

since he became CEO.

But sleep rarely came again

having been hijacked by images of

snakes, leopards, lizards, tigers

every member of his Board—

and an especially haunting hyena

with his mother's face,

and her endless ferocity.

Duplicity

At the end of his career
still pulsing with charisma
and other savored effects,
he was revealed to be
the duplicitous man
he had always been.

Hungry, savage swiftness
a torrential flooding of truth
sliced open his marriage—
its innards shredded,
bloodied masses of knowing
blocking every pathway around them.

Then, an ambivalently welcomed "then" later,
his days just emptied out—zombie trance
tracing his life with ghosts now, ghosts
staring out from photos askew on the piano
piano unable to play even one sweet reverie
for ghosts—gnawing at the edges of his sobriety.

The Corporate ABCs

Amazons join the gladiators now
Battle-scarred and proven
Corporate-crusted and as
Darwinian in pursuit of their results
Exceptional results
Fiercer and fiercer the stretch
Goals in a symbiotic dancing with
Habits—tribal habits
Indigenous as the
Just-in-time apologies offered to
Keep the family steady … everyone still in
Love enough even when the
Milestone events are missed
Never to be seen again because work
Obligations will usually trump the
Possibility of
Quality time with a child—or other close
Relation. Amazons need sleep but
Sleep isn't working as they are
Turning into cold backs … backs that trigger
Uneasy promises and everyone's
Very
Weary of the deepening chill
Xylophone shrill ringing through their beds as another
Year of promises adds up to
Zero.

Venezia, Last Visit With Peggy Guggenheim

In the palazzo courtyard
There
sudden words seen
living on the surface of a stone:

Savor kindness
Because
Cruelty is
Always
Possible later.

Was it there
There
that I witnessed your
most
serious
… reflection?

Scorpion Dance

One wore Teflon, the other quill

one used power, the other will

not cease his admonishments

even when summoned

into the stiffened silence

where he sparred anew

not seeing his blood ·

had already splattered

on the patterned runway

to the inner sanctum.

Neglected

The nest is more glass than twig now
no velvet berth for resting;
and the quiet is shrill, their evasions at a crescendo
stark kaleidoscope on the walls,
the walls that are converging
and resisting all paint,
they are dank from neglect
they cannot be painted over—
it is time for the conversation.

The walls are converging
they will not be painted,
they are soaked and keep weeping;
the tears on the floor form pools
the pools glow in the night from flies
green flies surround them at night …
there is no sleeping
only the blinking of flies reminding them
that it is time for the conversation.

But the conversation is always
swallowed before it's begun
dragged under as the house shudders
another convulsive grunt of absence
incrementally grooved by their busyness.
Quiet the fierce enemy now

it drapes over them ... soaken blanket of tears
and flies—flies watching their footsteps,
each person listening for the other
lest they meet in the quiet,
at the end of the hall,
where the wall has crumbled
and the flies have nested
in the place where he and she
will have to start the conversation,
each has dreaded for years.

Emperor's Jacket

The thickening quiet and ice—he could not know

what lay on the new path before him or who,

hidden in the bracken, awaited his trial there.

He did not see that the emperor's silk jacket

was really knotted and spotted with mud …

it had felt so smooth and generous at the table

when they beckoned each other into a union

of lasting effects.

He had not seen the photos of prey dripping

blood from the tiger's mouth on the wall there

blood that would soon intermingle with his—he

careening in a mire barely half his own making.

Scorched In Paradiso

1.

Rarely satisfied by day

he takes his need into the night

he works it hard into the night

his patina of grace and charm

splaying his prey open

pushing it around on the carpet

feeding it royal grapes and tuna;

he is weaving their thoughts together

heaping rewards, whispering the future

he is smoothing its fur, smelling its possibility ...

(has he not wearied of this repetition?).

2.

Later, the eruption ... inexplicable ice and thrust;

he is done feeding here

his sudden slinging of slime

toxic sludge of words

searing at the dinner table

in a place with a name like heaven.

Jekyl and Hyde squared

slime slung in a mass relentless

flattening his prey on the carpet

foot pressing its throat,

there is no air here—only the stench of his monstrosity.

The night is dead.

He is finished with it.

Drunk and black-hearted

barricaded in the back of a taxi

sent home, he's ready for sleep …

Oblivious.

3.

Postscript:

… and when finally he sighted the snow leopard,

she, startled still on the path before him,

he, near blinded and frozen over …

she opened her coat to receive him.

But inside her warmth, he flooded with drink

and set to re-freezing—seizing his dark tumble down

black hearted way again, full flight and fierce again

fierce silent rage colliding, sliding him down again

but then lifted—this time lifted by the white butterflies

she sent to save him.

Lahore 2006

Dust and trash intermingle with the scent of time here
dignity and grace infuse it further, seductive bouquet
as the businessmen sit on silk divans doing business
sipping tea—sidelong glances, white towels for sweat.

Sweat drips from others, too—the men pulling hay;
hard, serpentine pulling of hay
around animals and merchants
tireless pulling as the hay falls on the dirt,
this dirt the road
of the road more traveled—but without signpost or lane.

She takes this road to the border,
border where the soldiers strut at sunset
strutting for the people waving flags
people waving flags on both sides of the border
flags defiant in more distance than possibility.

Throngs on both sides of the border are roaring
fist-pumping, twirling and whirling for their nations
their nations where there is more dirt than truth,
more hype than stability, more plots than sanity,
and soon, more blood in the dirt near the border
the border where the strutting goes on unabated
as the businessmen keep on with their business and tea.

III.
TOXIC
Leaders

Killing Pigs

He took them to a place

where they chased wild pigs,

wrestled them to the ground,

and slit their throats dead.

Blood-smeared and breathless,

now this was a team

building.

Whip Lash

Beware the chameleon

straddling his branch as a throne

coral charm by day,

green in the twilight of nights after

he's feasted on the young learning to climb.

He'll swallow some whole whilst

beckoning their strides forward;

he'll ground others into paste when they falter,

… and still others, the more brightly-tinted than he,

will be whipped until they lay flattened and colorless.

Cracking Tension

A hidden He was revealed

the rare times he laughed fully—sudden stars leaping

from his throat

and cracking the tension he

spread over their meetings like sleet.

They wanted to freeze dry that laughter,

grind it into granules of hope stored in a jar

for liberal scooping into his morning coffee.

Dirt Trader

He trades in dirt,

leaving fetid lumps

on the rugs

at the top

of the tower

tracks of his truth

hot from the trenches.

They are impatient for him to finish.

Spin Me

I saw the monster
sudden radioactive glint
from the corner office
terror and toxin
spreading
people walking backwards
in the tangled quiet
contamination spreading
spreading fast
to the wires
wires now stripped down
Stark
to the truth …
truth tinder box
tinder box of truth
ignited, and he's revealed;
but he'll not tolerate
this intrusion. He
strikes another flame
his spinning top ablaze now
furious burn … to ashes
destruction enough
to satisfy
his ravenous delusion.

Cracked

There is a crack in his head

his head has a crack

a crack full of crackers

clogging his thinking with crumbs

crumbs falling out of his head

onto the floor, over the desks

and the chairs of his company

abundance of dirt

and egg shells … hip deep in egg shells and dirt.

They pull on their armor, navy wool gabardine

brushed clean in steel spinning booths;

they strap into the spinning booths daily—

furious turning as the brushes

clean and baste them in revision enough

for King Crumb to bind them in promises.

There is more dirt than reason,

more crackers than time,

more time than truth;

most are too stuffed to move

but the others …

the others have opted for sanity.

Stranded

If you went to the roof of his building at night
lantern lit, swinging it once to the left and three
to the right,
they would signal back once to the left and three
to the right
over and over these low stars on the sea
shooting once to the left and three
to the right
these stranded workers on ice, no possibility—but to
wait for the light once to the left and three
to the right
ready again—for him to feed of their waning vitality.

Hard Body

Hard Body bursts into the night he calls morning,

grasping his tools of construction

embracing each as a lover ...

grunts and sweat as a lover in rain,

sweat dripping like rain

profusion of rain and profanity,

washing over his skin as he locks on

the man in the mirror,

true lover in the mirror

mirror his most fervent lover

aroused in the bulge of his efforts ...

exhorting his combat with time.

Crash

1.

Crabs, hornets, hawks,
tigers, bats, and bees –
all manner of talon and sting
crowd this inner space,
fragile sum of himself invented.
No amount of recognition
can quell the cacophony here,
not even death's warning
could ease the tidal effects
of his self perfection.

2.

So that sudden blink of sleep
then the hurling forward,
shrieking smack of steel
into the torso of an ancient tree
a mile from home,
ignited his particular indignation.

Thick, black, bloodied night
metallic taste, silent terror
belief and disbelief
relief and rage
shame and repulsion
all intermingled
in the destructed hulk.

His body slacked into the air bag
oblivious to the horn's bleating,
the shards of glass gleaming,
the ants recovering their wounded,
a paralyzed rabbit whimpering,
the grasses beaten into paste.

3.

Days upon days later the oft-repeated story
still expanded and shrunk
from the invisible breathing bag
heaving inexplicably at his side
in the office
outside the Board room
at the executive dining table –
a relentless wheezing
deterring his efforts
to repress the imperfect event.

4.

Even the flooding of flashbacks
soaking the bed sheets each night,
intruding into meetings most days,
this kaleidic glimpse of an end
triggered only
his hardened retreat into the familiar,

a dismissal of the fright,
a revision of the event
and, inevitably,
the purchase of an even bigger ride.

Friendless

It's hard to work for a man with no friends;
there's not enough air or light
between when he comes and goes
for the office to thrive in its busyness.
There's not enough safety to be foolish
or enough shared history to trust in the future.

What's in the heart of a man without friends?
Mother's stiffened back
Father's preoccupations
A brother's jeering laughter
A sister's red sweater
The bully's taunting?

Perhaps it's unpopped kernels of corn
tiger eye marbles
or bits of licorice all stuck in a lump
or the smell of school thick with boredom and dread.

Is it the darkened parlor where the guests never came
too much playing alone in the basement
or memory of the girl who winced running
when he tried to kiss her?

Maybe it's just the comfort of quiet
or that no one ever said his name
with enough enthusiasm for him to want to answer.
Perhaps it's the images of loves craved and destroyed
countless half starts turned into charcoal but never lit?

Friendless ... he ensured the chill,
the weariness of every morning,
the escape of every night.
He perpetuated the blandness
so thick that even the evening cleaning crew
could not clear it.

The Prince of Dole

A Fairy Tale of Serious Proportion

The Prince of Dole ruled the most prosperous region within a land of abundance, but he was more revered for his brilliance than loved by his subjects. His enigmatic and moody ways confused many about his expectations and how they could ever please him fully. Still others resented how he swung between hostile neglect and charming manipulation. And everyone in the palace knew to avoid the Prince in the evenings when his enormous consumption of wine influenced his most unkind and vile behavior.

Because the Prince of Dole was somewhat aware of his limitations as a ruler and had an even clearer understanding of whom he needed to make his region prosper, he established a secret fund. From this fund, the Prince showered unexpected largesse with the expectation that this would ensure the allegiance, admiration, and hard work of his most talented subjects. This cache of potential rewards was overseen by his most trusted knight—the only knight who escaped the Prince's stinging words and chaotic ramblings about the future of the kingdom.

So satisfied was the Prince by the seeming effects of his beneficence, he did not see that even as his subjects fed of his favors, they discerned the truth of his intention. Silently they avoided being pulled into the spider of him. They denied him access to their best thinking—reserving that for the Princes of other regions who urged them to cross the moat. They also countered the Prince's efforts to blame or label them as incompetent when the King railed about their failures. And mostly, they bonded together in an unspoken covenant to survive the Prince's worst paranoid and self-serving effects.

In the end, the Prince of Dole did not live happily ever after—especially once he had depleted the fund for enticing both his subjects and close family members. Under darkness he left the kingdom settling finally into a remote place barren of lanterns or song. And while never missed as ruler, or lover, or friend, his wounding effects on others converted into luminous lessons about leadership and love. Most significantly, what they had learned about the limits of financial manipulation and inconstant relationships served them well with every other Prince thereafter.

Commentaries on Poems

The Solidity of Fog

27

In Asia for the first time, this executive finds himself in the grip of its unfamiliarity and enigmatic beauty—both rolling over him as a fog. Despite the urgency of the business issues he must resolve there, he remains calm and resolute relying on his strengths, experiences, and instincts to find his way through the challenges before him.

Deal Weaver

29

The CEO subject of this poem is intent upon making a key acquisition. At the end of a critical dinner meeting, he catches a word of ambivalence uttered mistakenly by someone representing the other side. By morning, the potential buyer has channeled his business acumen and interpersonal skills in a manner that keeps the deal moving forward.

Boss Titillated

31

In this power role reversal scenario, a female executive becomes physically attracted to one of her direct reports. Briefly swept up in the pleasure of her fantasy about him, she must revert to the combination of her common sense, political instincts, and ambition to avoid making a career-limiting mistake.

Killer Bees

33

Physically abused by his father as a child, the underlying murderous rage of this executive is revealed through a dream. Discussion of this dream with his executive coach yielded both cathartic and insight-oriented effects—especially in terms of his difficulty with fully trusting others, and the revengeful reactions he could have toward authority figures at work who disagreed with him.

On the River

35

Having struggled with the decision to retire, this corporate lawyer suffered no loss of identity or depressive effects that can typify this life stage transition. On the contrary, he felt relieved, revived, resuscitated. He found his new life rhythm quickly—abetted by engaging non-work-related interests and the fact that his positive sense of self was not dependent upon the continuance of his career.

Biscuit

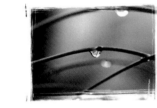

37

Despite the strain of frequent and long business travel, this husband and wife stayed focused on maintaining their version of work-family integration. In doing so, they minimized the feelings of emptiness and alienation that can erode the quality and stability of many executive couple relationships—especially once they reach retirement.

Mourning in Kyoto

39

The generosity of an emotionally attuned boss helped one of his direct reports mourn the loss of her husband. Knowing that she was a gardener, he encouraged the inclusion of Kyoto in a business trip she took to Asia. While walking the gardens there, she began a journey back to herself—a self that still embraced her marital identity but also started to become distinct from it.

Empty Next

41

This CEO of a non-for-profit organization wrestled with the conundrum of meaning exacerbated by "empty nest" feelings—intense feelings triggered by her younger child leaving for college. Her Freudian slip of "next" for "nest" opened a conversation with the author about legacy. In the wake of this important conversation, she discovered new meaning through the identification of a few compelling life goals—and her explicit planning for how to achieve them.

Standing on Marbles

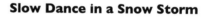

43

Even as women continue to secure top corporate jobs, certain stereotypes about them persist. These stereotypes—most often related to hard-charging ambition and aggressive determination—can overwhelm adequate appreciation of a distinctive leadership strength: the ability to achieve stellar results by blending their aggression, multi-tasking, toughness, and interpersonal warmth.

Slow Dance in a Snow Storm

44

The fatigue and tedium of global business travel can be intensified by the repetitive, predictable conversations that occur among business colleagues as they wait for the flight to their next destination. While this female executive may have appeared distracted to her travel companions, the constructive value of reverie as a productive distraction, an energizer, and a haven of relief is illustrated here through her memories of a former lover.

Duende

46

With his duende—Spanish for personal magnetism and charm—this senior executive has eased his direct report's anxiety and turned the annual performance review into a rare and inspirational conversation. This conversation is anchored in an atmosphere of hope and passion about the future … a future they will create together. In the fading light of this important afternoon, there is a fierceness about the power of candor and clarity. We are reminded that the most remarkable leaders are inspirational, open, and strive to ignite excitement and alignment with the people whom they lead.

PERILOUS LEADERS

Riffed Off

50

As the model of lifetime employment in one company dies, long term employees are being emptied out of their offices at a rapid clip. For many this is experienced as an abysmal, irreconcilable loss of identity. Some recover finding solace in the warmth of loved ones and other ways to use their skills and experiences. Others never quite recover and like the executive in this poem, they sink into depression, isolate themselves in self-pitying shame, and attempt to deaden their pain with alcohol..

Night Moves

53

Having become CEO of a company under siege given bad market conditions and with a challenging Board of Directors, this executive's stress was exacerbated further by his mother's relentless demands and inability to affirm his long-sought accomplishment. At odds with key members of his leadership team and living away from his family, this executive drank excessively which further reinforced his sense of isolation.

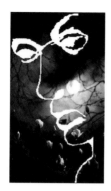

Duplicity

The "double life" of this talented business man was revealed just as he retired from a long and successful career with a global company. Despite efforts to repair the emotional damage done to his wife of 30+ years—efforts that included his participation in a residential treatment program for sex and alcohol addiction, this marriage was destroyed. His transition into retirement became both a literal and figurative starting over.

The Corporate ABCs

While the number of female executives in top corporate roles has yet to approximate that of males, this number is trending upward. From a work-family integration perspective what we see in the lives of these successful women parallels the lives of their male peers: the intensity of trying to juggle both spheres of life, and the inevitable resentments that can accrue over time.

Venezia, Last Visit With Peggy Guggenheim

In the courtyard of Peggy Guggenheim's Venetian palazzo is a stone carved with a few simple albeit inspirational words. These words caught the attention of the Managing Partner of a U.S. law firm who stopped to read them aloud and then recited them later at a luncheon with friends. In this vignette, we are reminded of the power of seizing an unexpected moment, of how such moments can ignite conversation, and of the importance of reflection.

The numbers 54, 57, and 58 appear to the left of each section.

Scorpion Dance

61

While courageous truth-telling can show up on the leadership competency lists of companies intent on developing stellar leaders, there is often a gap between the intention of this competency and its manifestation in business life. Truth tellers can get labeled as renegades, rabble rousers, or malcontents—unless they study the targets of their truth-telling exceedingly well. This scrutiny must include choosing the right times and places to say what needs to be heard. Unfortunately, the protagonist in this poem did not do so and was ultimately fired by his boss who was one of the top five corporate executives in this global enterprise.

Neglected

62

Given the stress and resentment that can build incrementally in the life of an executive couple, making time for empathic communication is critical to marital health and happiness. However, such communication is more likely delayed or avoided. In this poem, a couple, now empty nesters, can no longer escape the need to talk but they are ill-equipped to begin the conversation.

Emperor's Jacket

65

Too often companies experience negative hiring outcomes because they fail to assimilate or "on board" new hires. In "Emperor's Jacket" we see this problem play out in an alpha male culture in which outsiders must prove themselves quickly before receiving any measure of respect or collegiality. The problem is exacerbated further by a General Manager with a penchant for hiring atypical job candidates—and by a candidate who was not a good match for the job but who nevertheless allowed himself to be lured into it by his boss's charismatic persuasion.

Scorched in Paradiso

66

The seduction and abandonment behavior pattern of a brilliant business Vice President takes its ugliest turn suddenly at the table in a public restaurant. Despite his unpredictable mood swings, chronic feelings of emptiness, punishing treatment of others, and excessive drinking, he ran a successful business in a competitive marketplace where his reflexive aggression and paranoia paid off. The stunned target of his hostility chooses to help rather than to flee from him. But it is unlikely that he will be helped—absent his serious intention to change and his seeking the necessary psychological assistance to do so.

Lahore 2006

71

The "she" in Lahore 2006 is a Pakistani manager in an American-owned manufacturing company. Through her eyes we are reminded that commerce can continue—and thrive—even in the midst of political chaos and significant poverty. We are reminded, too of how successful business executives honor and participate in local customs and, how they may bear discomfort and danger as they pursue their work-related objectives.

TOXIC LEADERS

Killing Pigs

74

The motivation of this sales executive was to provide a "memorable" team-building experience for his all-male team—an experience that would "surpass anything" they had ever done before. This florid example of bad judgment, fuelled by a leader's narcissism and negligible understanding of how to build a strong team, also raises serious questions about his suitability for leadership responsibility.

Whip Lash

Brilliant at recruiting top talent, this gifted but insecure entrepreneur found overt or covert ways to squash the spirit of anyone who threatened his ego. Even the compelling need for him to retain the talented people he hired so his fledgling consulting firm could flourish did not neutralize the adverse effects of his deep-seated psychological issues.

Cracking Tension

For some executives, the need to achieve, strive for perfection, and dominate the competition are so deeply embedded in their personalities that they just can't lighten up. They not only can't relax, they won't because they believe their relentless and stern discipline is at the core of their effectiveness. This is bad news for their teams because how they perform is a narcissistic extension of such leaders. For these driven executives, rarely is anything ever good enough and thus their teams are mired in chronic feelings of tension, intimidation, resentment, and fatigue.

Dirt Trader

Company gossip mongers are Company gossip mongers are an ever present and dangerous business reality. Whatever their real jobs may be, they primarily seek and survive on the bits of social trash they carry to people in power who will listen. As distasteful as the experience can be, senior executives will give them audience, they will listen because it is politically wise to spend just the right amount of time with them—no more, no less.

Spin Me

Despite the widespread use of 360-feedback and its proven value as a leadership development tool, many executives are not open to information that challenges the persona they have carefully crafted from the outset of a career. Along with the persona comes a thick set of defenses to protect it. These defenses include denial, withdrawal, and rationalization. "Spin Me" captures a leader's instantaneous fury about—and burning need to defend against—the constructive feedback given him by his Human Resources Vice President.

Cracked

Some senior executives leaders have psychiatric disorders. While rare in large, public companies, it is not uncommon in privately-held enterprises. In these contexts, there can be brilliant founder/owners or second or third generation family members with diagnosable psychological problems. With no one to whom they must report, no scrutiny of a Board of Directors, these leaders can wreak constant emotional havoc.

Stranded

Metaphorically speaking, there are leaders who fall in and out of love with their employees. As a Vice President in a career consulting firm once said of its founder and CEO, "One day you're up with him and the next you could be in Siberia." This behavior is common among individuals with significant mood swings and those with a bottomless need for ego-feeding. The emotionally cold boss in this poem perpetuates a pattern of sending employees to their metaphorical Siberia—and then re-instating them at will.

82

84

86

89

Hard Body

In Hard Body we meet an executive whose preoccupation with his physical appearance and strength requires a daily schedule that revolves around his gym work-outs. The obsessive need to preserve his physical appeal and power trumps everything else. Further, his remaining a "hard body" is an unconscious defense against his greatest fear: death.

Crash

91

Like many business executives, the subject of this poem defines himself exclusively by his work and particularly by his herculean 24x7 work ethic. Therefore nothing—not even a close death experience—would trigger introspection about his work habits. He was, in fact, more embarrassed than concerned about his car accident. It represented an error on his part, a sudden intrusion, and an untidiness in his otherwise neat and controlled existence, one he fought hard to repress.

Friendless

94

For business leaders who lack substantive friendships either within or outside of work, relationships are primarily transactional versus personal. These leaders remain focused on the objectives to be met and make minimal, if any, effort to learn about the lives of those with whom they work. This way of relating to others fuels a mood of serious quiet at work—an atmosphere lacking in the open exchange of ideas and the fun of creative collaboration.

The Prince Of Dole: A Fairy Tale of Serious Proportion

Certain business executives, especially those who lack the charisma and authenticity to motivate and inspire others, will use financial incentives and/or other "perks" to retain and ensure the committed efforts of their best employees. Limited in their capacity for emotional closeness and constancy, they can also repeat this pattern with family members whom they manipulate and make beholden to them financially. What these leaders choose to see as loyalty is often unspoken resentment—or worse.

97

Artist's Statement & Biographies

Richard McKnight

Richard McKnight is the author of *Victim, Survivor, or Navigator? Choosing a Response to Workplace Change*, and the co-author of *Leading Strategy Execution*. In addition to being a writer and artist, he is a publisher and organizational consultant (see TrueNorthPress.com and McKnightKaney.com). In the latter capacity, Rick consults with senior executives on business strategy and its execution. Rick has a PhD in organizational psychology in addition to a Bachelor's degree in Art.

WHEN I WAS FIRST INTRODUCED to Karol, she mentioned that she was a poet. Even before I had read any of her poetry, I knew I wanted to do a book project with her and said so. For one thing, her reputation preceded her; she was known to me as one of the best executive coaches on the east coast. For another, she impressed me immediately as a person of uncommon depth. And there was her *joie de vivre* (she would say *gioia di vivere* since she speaks Italian). We would make a very good team, I thought, so I courted her vigorously, typesetting some of her poems and illustrating them with my images as a means of enticing her.

It was a year before Karol was ready to collaborate on the project I had in mind. In the interim, she wrote a prose book on the subject of leadership types (*Behind the Executive Door*, Springer-Verlag). I was delighted when she came back to me with an invitation to collaborate on this illustrated volume.

Some of the images you see here were created before Karol and I met, others were created expressly for this project. Some of the images you see here are straight photography (e.g., pp. 14, 40, and—believe it or not—p. 67), but most are composites, i.e., pictures made up of two or more images.

For the composited pieces, I begin with an image that intrigues me and then embellish it with other images or parts of images to make the statement. The images are blended together digitally in Photoshop. A complex image is on p. 34 ("Killer Bees"). It has fourteen layers, i.e., fragments of different photographs combined to make the image.

Typically, when producing my art, I do not have an end in mind, rather I strive for a result that is both beautiful and edgy, sweet and disturbing, mirroring how I see life itself. Most of my images are surreal, i.e., a blend of the actual and the imagined, the abstract and the literal, the sublime and the ridiculous.

A dear friend is fond of saying that corporate life is not for the faint of heart. As representative of that life, Karol's poems are not for the faint of heart, either. As I read them, I experience the longing, imperfection, striving, and even cruelty that corporate executives can evince. Leaders, even the remarkable and kindly ones, can—and sometimes must—drive, push, judge, rip, and tear. But even ruthless leaders can take others to a desirable future and create organizations that sing, and often do.

I have meant for these glorious and terrible effects to be visible in my imagery, which is at once sweet (the colors) and sobering (the content). While they are often dark and perilous, my images, like businesses, are never drab.

The poet Mary Oliver once wrote, "Every day I see or hear something that nearly kills me with delight." I would like my imagery to have that effect. When people see my work, my fervent hope is that they become caught up for a moment in a place that has no words, a place filled with wonder, awe, and harmony—even if what they're looking at is that picture of those skulls on p. 84. I want to stop people in their tracks.

Many of these images are available as fine art prints at
RichardMcKnight.com.

Karol M. Wasylyshyn

THE CHILD OF POLISH IMMIGRANTS, I grew up in an ethnic enclave where my first job in life was to be the culture guide—the eyes and ears—for my working class relatives. It's no accident then that my career pursuits–journalist, clinical psychologist, consultant, and entrepreneur—have all involved the seeing and hearing of others in ways that fuelled our mutual understanding and success. While these work experiences have been a necessary prelude to this book, it is the deeply personal connections allowed me by my clients, and my growing desire to give away psychology to a broader audience that enabled the writing of *Standing on Marbles*.

With *Standing on Marbles* I tried to harness—in an instructive and attuned manner—the glitter and the gauntlets of executive life, the tales of promise and peril, and the fears that pursue business leaders like hungry wolves in the wood. By condensing many of my engagements into poems, I hoped to pull the reader quickly into these cases where they could absorb the psychological insights in them and use those insights for an enriched understanding about leaders—good and bad. I wanted these poems, or executive vignettes as I sometimes call them, to have learning, affirming, surprising, and even searing effects on the reader. But it was not until I met Rick McKnight that I believed these effects could be fully realized. By merging Rick's images—his exquisite way of seeing—with my verse, we created a legacy piece of work that we hope has illuminated important truths about business leadership.

By training, I am a clinical psychologist with a background in business. I have spent nearly three decades consulting to senior executives in both public and privately-held business enterprises. A pioneer of executive coaching in the United States, I blend my expertise in human potential, behavior change, and emotional intelligence to ensure and advance the leadership effectiveness of top business executives. I have worked with executives representing every global sector in companies to include: Bristol-Myers Squibb, Colgate Palmolive, Dupont, FMC, GlaxoSmithKline, Henkels & McCoy, Johnson & Higgins (now Marsh), Norfolk Southern Railroad, Pfizer, PriceWaterhouseCoopers, Revlon, and Rohm and Haas (now Dow).

My next book, *Behind the Executive Door,* is also for the general public and will be published by Springer-Verlag in the winter of 2011. In this work, I will explore my three leadership types from a cognitive and analytical perspective and provide guidance intended to help others better manage bosses who represent these types.

NOTES

NOTES

We produce and market inspiring books for those who seek to embrace life enthusiastically, possess boundless vitality, and address challenges confidently. To inquire about bulk orders, visit us online at TrueNorthPress.com.

CPSIA information can be obtained
at www.ICGtesting.com
Printed in the USA
LVIC042038010312
271158LV00001B